Trace and Write
Numbers 1-100

Preschool | Kindergarten | 1st Grade | Beginning Writer Series

Over 1,200+ tracing units

for beginning writers!

Smart Kidz College

Trace numbers 1-10.

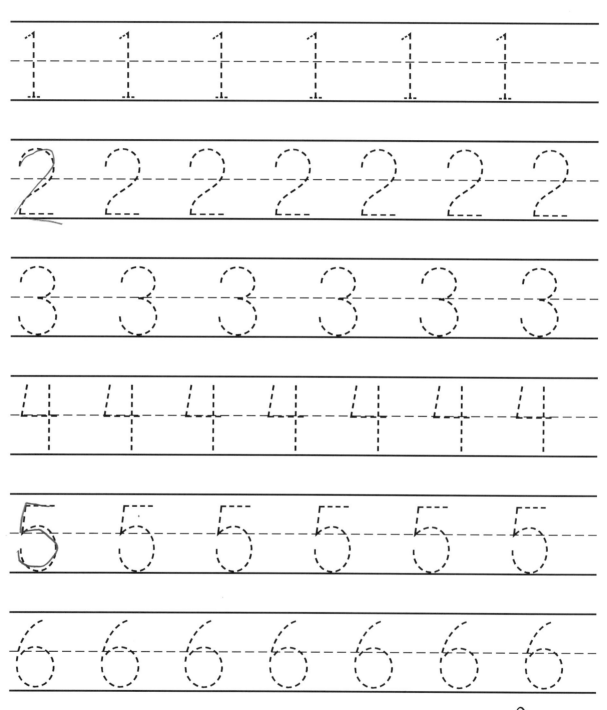

1 1 1 1 1 1 1

2 2 2 2 2 2 2

3 3 3 3 3 3 3

4 4 4 4 4 4 4

5 5 5 5 5 5 5

6 6 6 6 6 6 6

Trace and Write Numbers 1-100

Trace numbers 1-10.

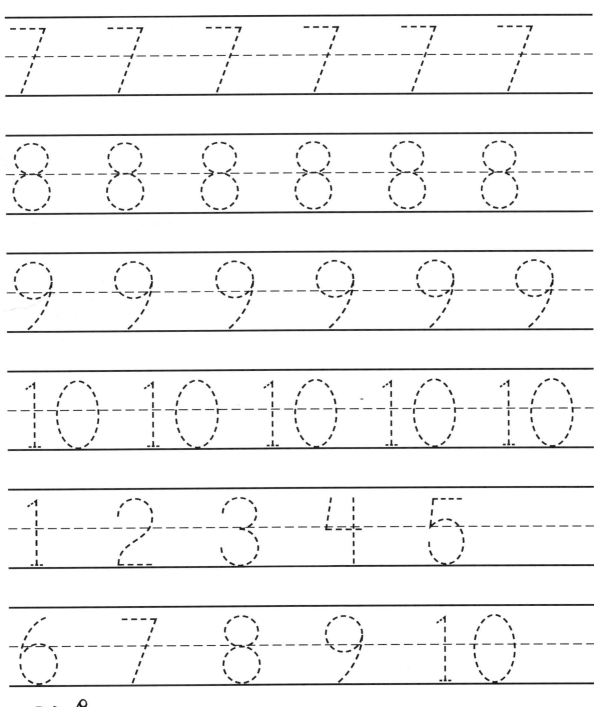

Trace and Write Numbers 1-100

Practice writing numbers 1-10.

1

2

3

4

5

1 2 3 4 5

Practice writing numbers 1-10.

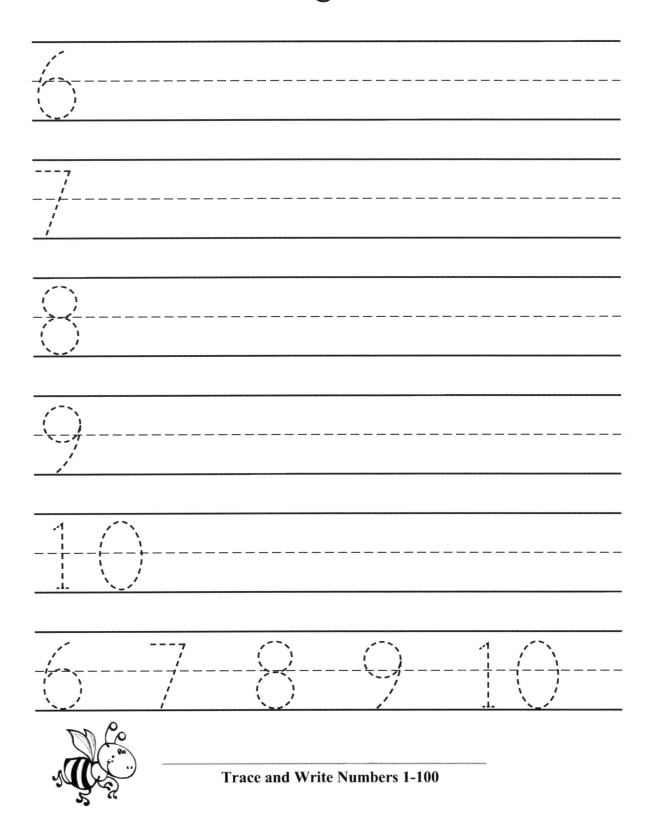

Trace and Write Numbers 1-100

Tracing & Writing Numbers 11-20

Trace numbers 11-20.

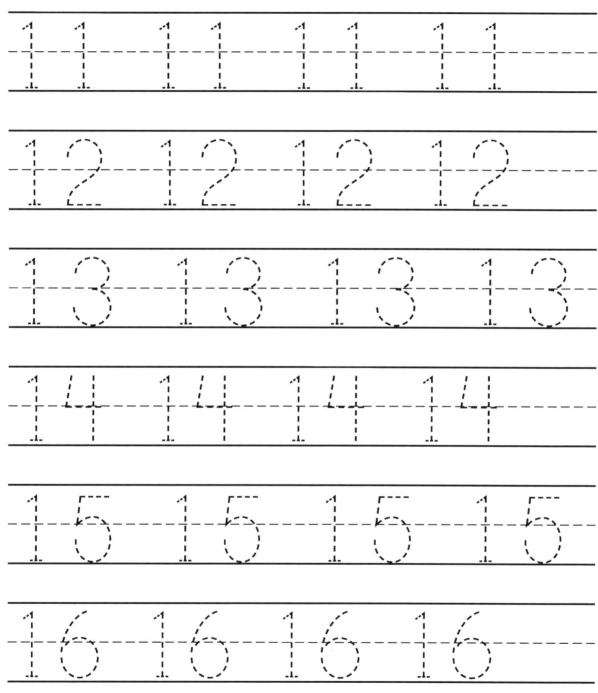

11 11 11 11 11 11 11 11

12 12 12 12 12

13 13 13 13 13

14 14 14 14 14

15 15 15 15 15

16 16 16 16 16

Trace and Write Numbers 1-100

Trace numbers 11-20.

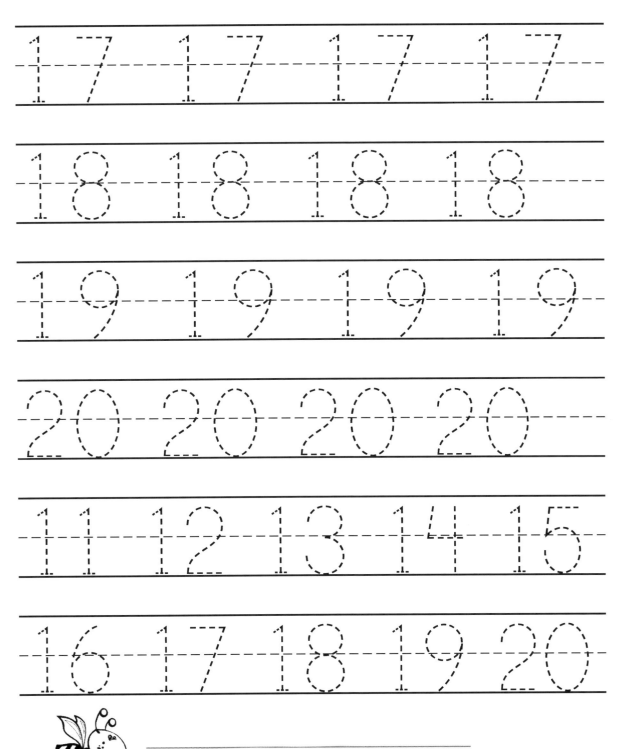

17 17 17 17 17 17

18 18 18 18 18

19 19 19 19 19

20 20 20 20 20

11 12 13 14 15

16 17 18 19 20

Trace and Write Numbers 1-100

Practice writing numbers 11-20.

11

12

13

14

15

11 12 13 14 15

Practice writing numbers 11-20.

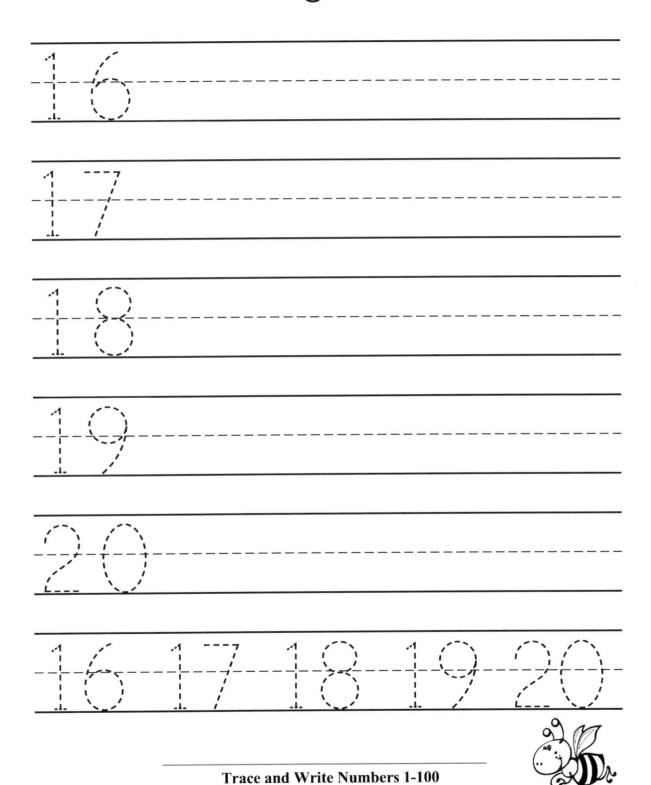

16

17

18

19

20

16 17 18 19 20

Trace and Write Numbers 1-100

Tracing & Writing Numbers 21-30

Trace numbers 21-30.

21 21 21 21 21 21

22 22 22 22 22 22

23 23 23 23 23

24 24 24 24 24

25 25 25 25 25

26 26 26 26 26

Trace and Write Numbers 1-100

Trace numbers 21-30.

27 27 27 27 27

28 28 28 28 28

29 29 29 29 29

30 30 30 30 30

21 22 23 24 25

26 27 28 29 30

Trace and Write Numbers 1-100

Practice writing numbers 21-30.

21

22

23

24

25

21 22 23 24 25

Practice writing numbers 21-30.

26 -----

27 -----

28 -----

29 -----

30 -----

26 27 28 29 30

Trace and Write Numbers 1-100

Tracing & Writing
Numbers 31-40

Trace numbers 31-40.

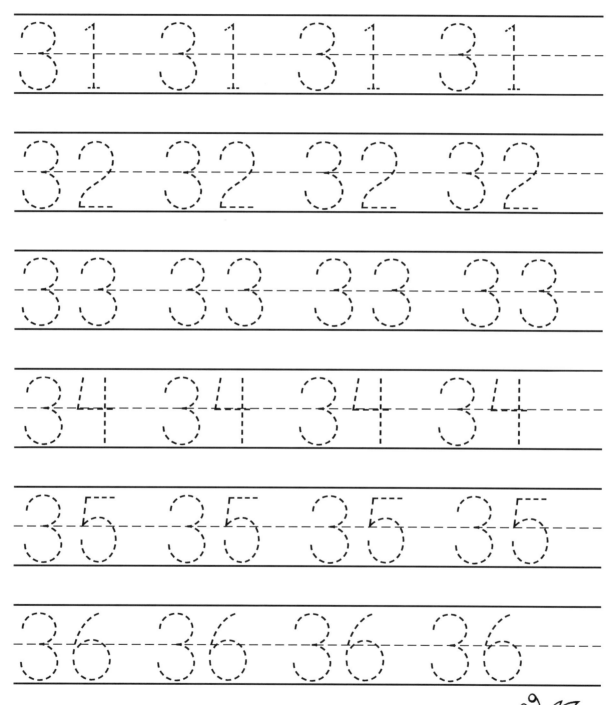

31 31 31 31 31

32 32 32 32 32

33 33 33 33 33

34 34 34 34 34

35 35 35 35 35

36 36 36 36 36

Trace numbers 31-40.

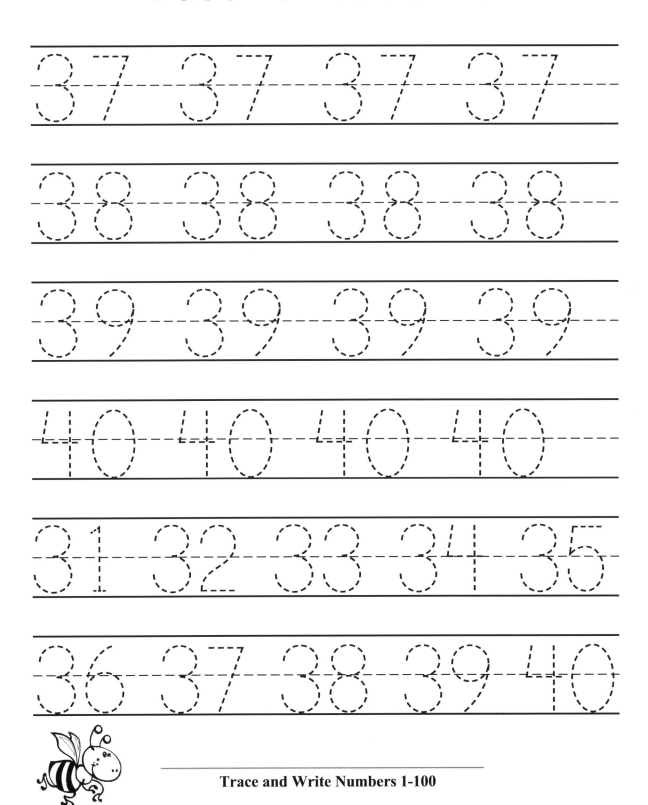

Trace and Write Numbers 1-100

Practice writing numbers 31-40.

3 1

3 2

3 3

3 4

3 5

31 32 33 34 35

Practice writing numbers 31-40.

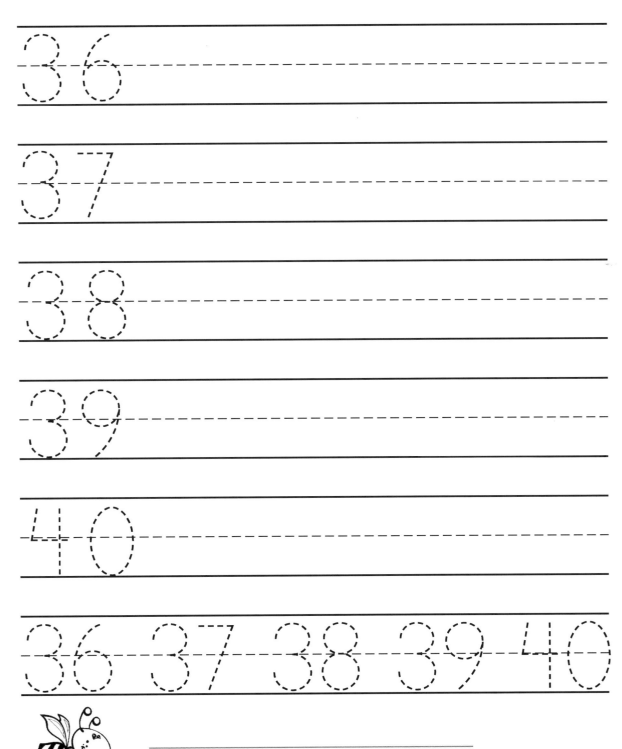

Trace and Write Numbers 1-100

Tracing & Writing Numbers 41-50

With Practice Review for 1-50

Trace numbers 41-50.

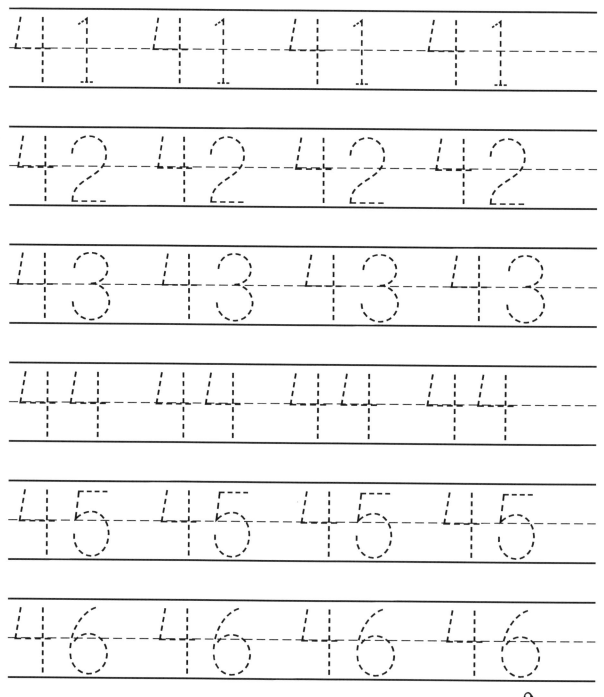

Trace numbers 41-50.

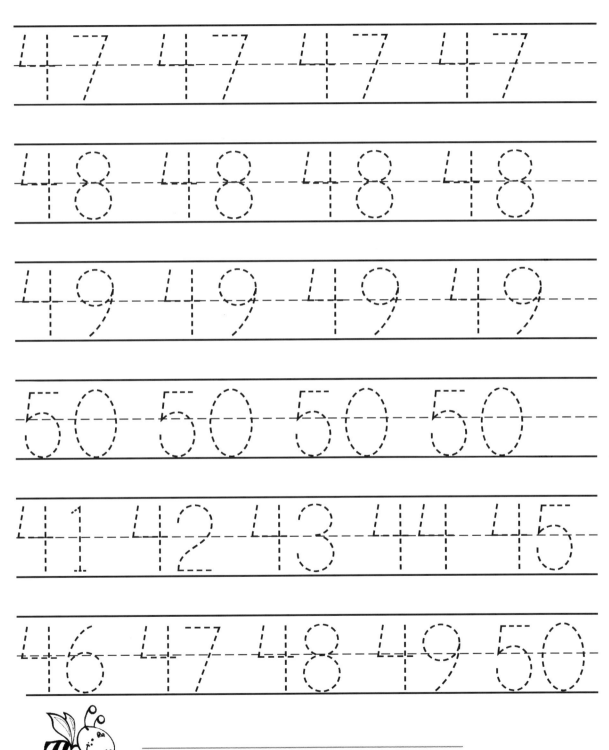

47 47 47 47

48 48 48 48

49 49 49 49

50 50 50 50

41 42 43 44 45

46 47 48 49 50

Trace and Write Numbers 1-100

Practice writing numbers 41-50.

41

42

43

44

45

41 42 43 44 45

Practice writing numbers 41-50.

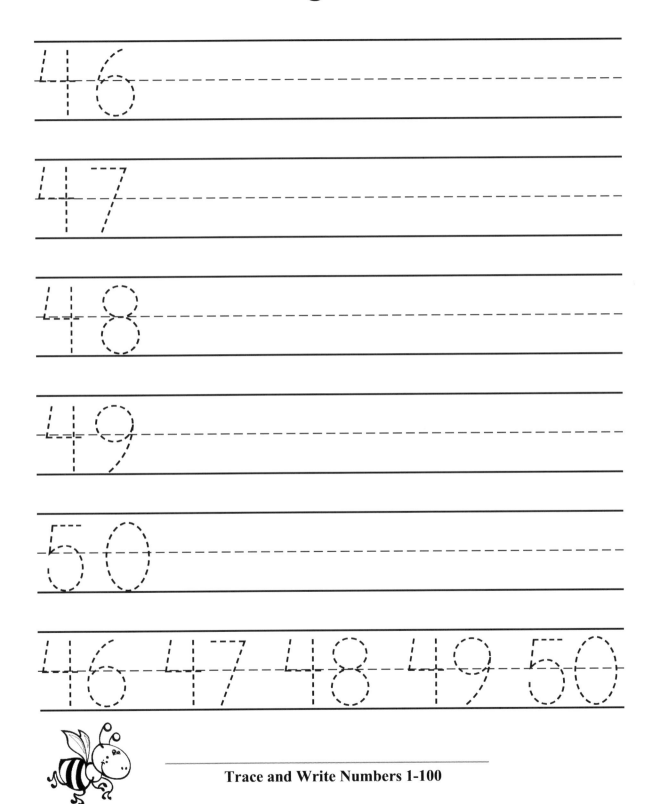

46

47

48

49

50

46 47 48 49 50

Trace and Write Numbers 1-100

Practice Review 1-50.

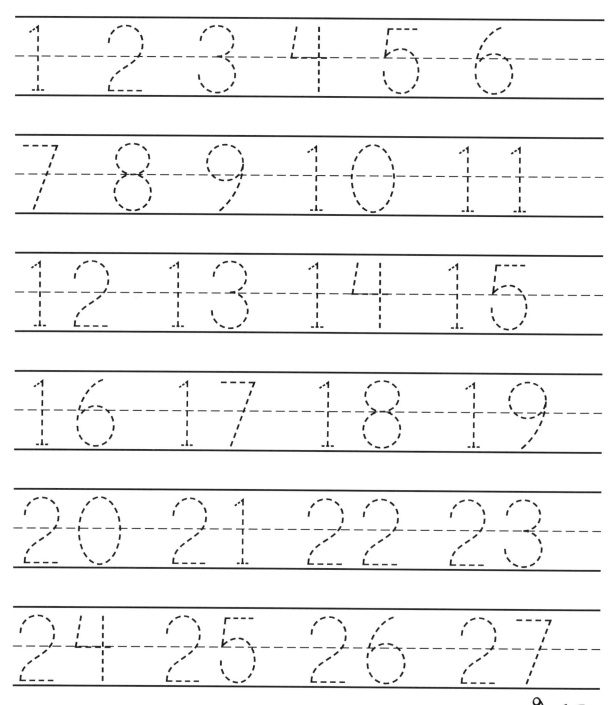

1 2 3 4 5 6

7 8 9 10 11

12 13 14 15

16 17 18 19

20 21 22 23

24 25 26 27

Trace and Write Numbers 1-100

Practice Review 1-50.

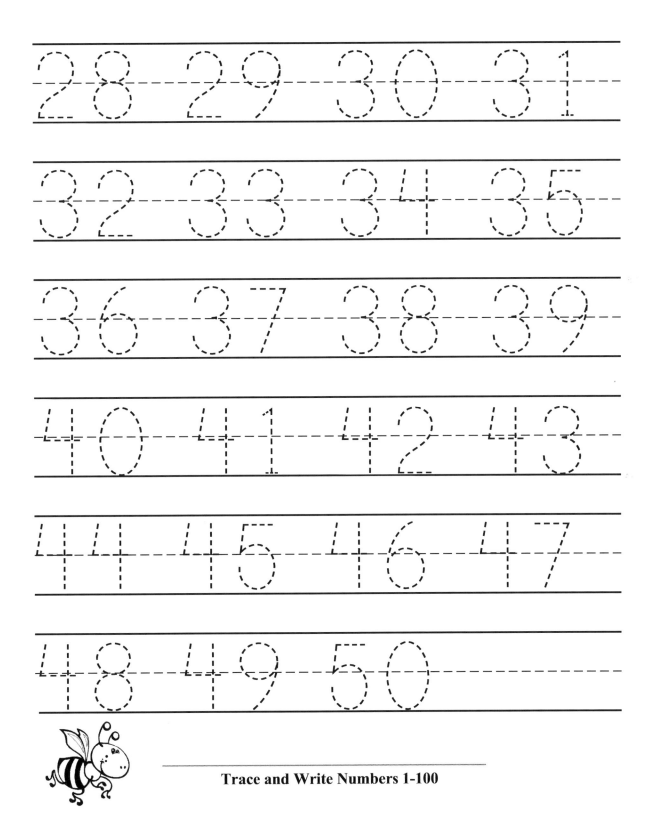

28 29 30 31

32 33 34 35

36 37 38 39

40 41 42 43

44 45 46 47

48 49 50

Trace and Write Numbers 1-100

Tracing & Writing Numbers 51-60

Trace numbers 51-60.

51 51 51 51 51

52 52 52 52

53 53 53 53

54 54 54 54

55 55 55 55

56 56 56 56

Trace numbers 51-60.

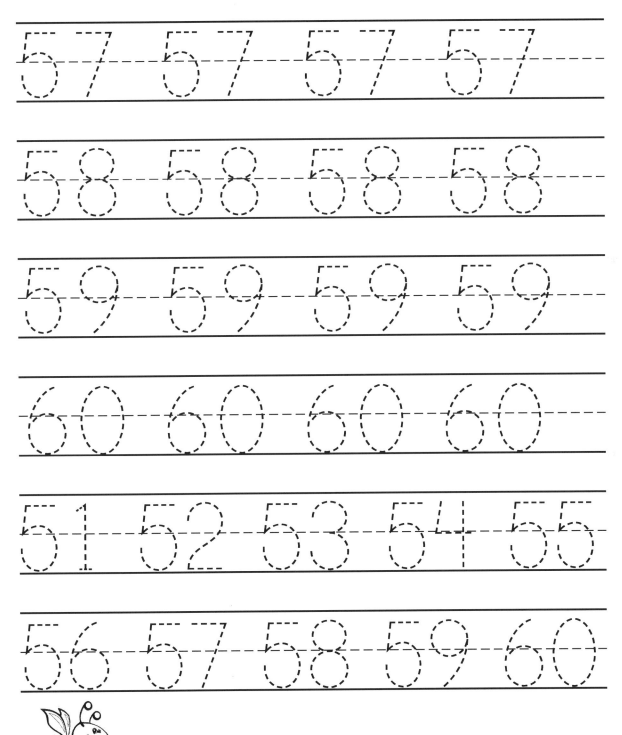

57 57 57 57 57

58 58 58 58 58

59 59 59 59 59

60 60 60 60 60

51 52 53 54 55

56 57 58 59 60

Trace and Write Numbers 1-100

Practice writing numbers 51-60.

51

52

53

54

55

51 52 53 54 55

Practice writing numbers 51-60.

56

57

58

59

60

56 57 58 59 60

Trace and Write Numbers 1-100

Tracing & Writing Numbers 61-70

Trace numbers 61-70.

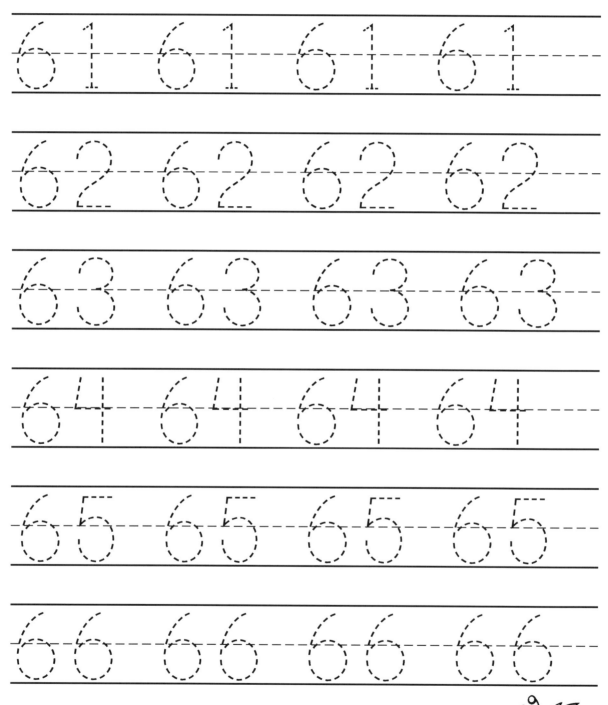

61 61 61 61 61

62 62 62 62

63 63 63 63

64 64 64 64

65 65 65 65

66 66 66 66

Trace numbers 61-70.

Practice writing numbers 61-70.

61

62

63

64

65

61 62 63 64 65

Practice writing numbers 61-70.

Trace and Write Numbers 1-100

Tracing & Writing Numbers 71-80

Trace numbers 71-80.

71 71 71 71 71

72 72 72 72 72

73 73 73 73 73

74 74 74 74 74

75 75 75 75 75

76 76 76 76 76

Trace and Write Numbers 1-100

Trace numbers 71-80.

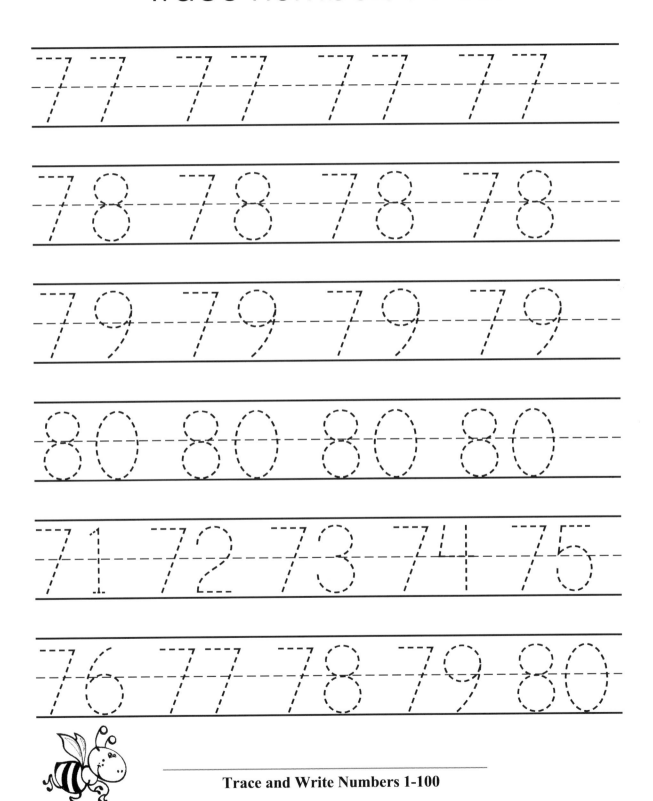

Trace and Write Numbers 1-100

Practice writing numbers 71-80.

71

72

73

74

75

71 72 73 74 75

Practice writing numbers 71-80.

Trace and Write Numbers 1-100

Tracing & Writing Numbers 81-90

Trace numbers 81-90.

81 81 81 81

82 82 82 82

83 83 83 83

84 84 84 84

85 85 85 85

86 86 86 86

Trace numbers 81-90.

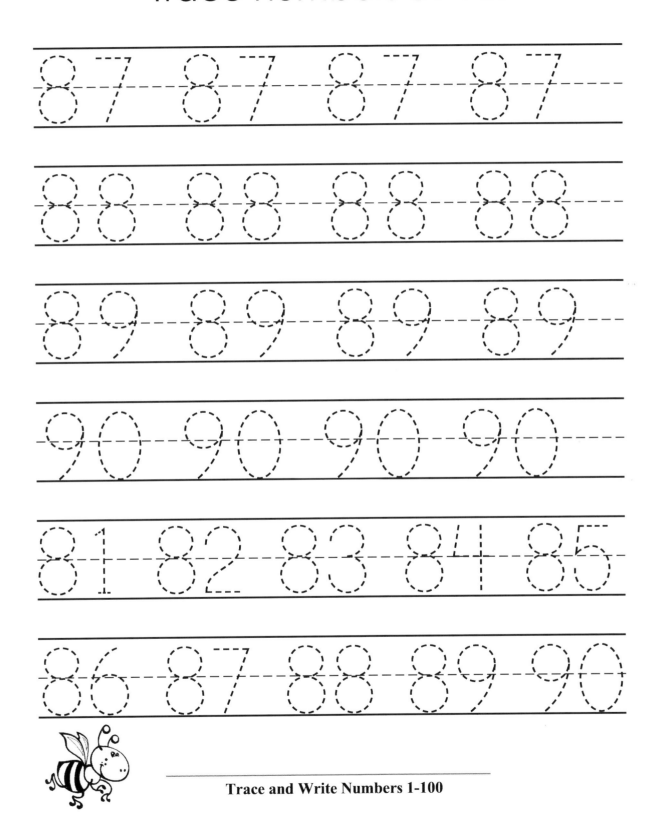

Trace and Write Numbers 1-100

Practice writing numbers 81-90.

81 ------------------------------------

82 ------------------------------------

83 ------------------------------------

84 ------------------------------------

85 ------------------------------------

81 82 83 84 85

Practice writing numbers 81-90.

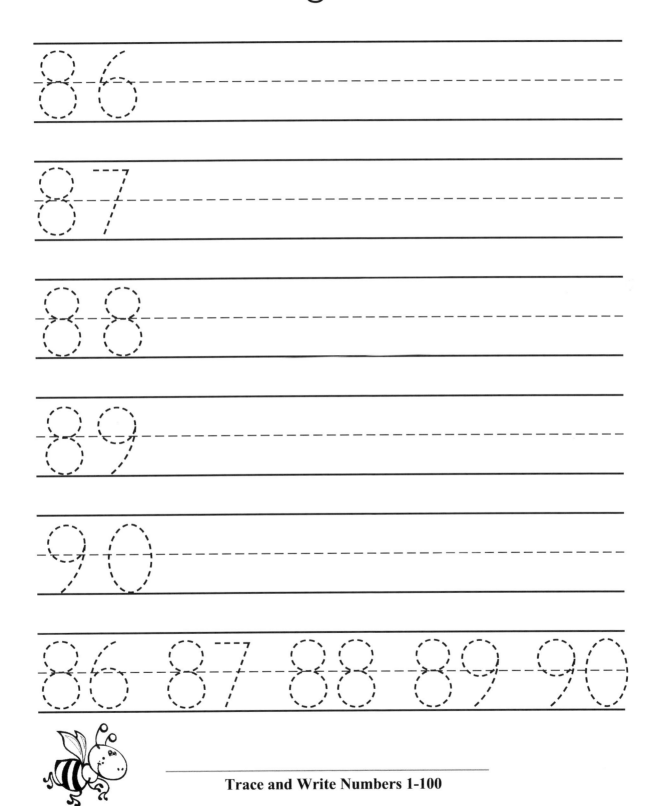

Trace and Write Numbers 1-100

Tracing & Writing Numbers 91-100

With Practice Review for 51-100

Trace numbers 91-100.

91 91 91 91 91

92 92 92 92 92

93 93 93 93 93

94 94 94 94 94

95 95 95 95 95

96 96 96 96 96

Trace numbers 91-100.

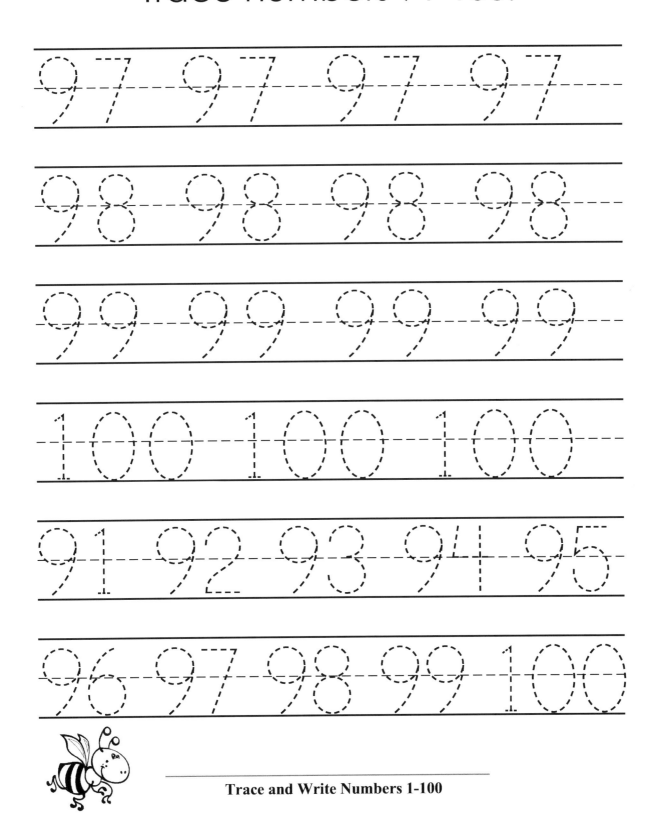

Trace and Write Numbers 1-100

Practice writing numbers 91-100.

9 1 -

9 2 -

9 3 -

9 4 -

9 5 -

9 1 9 2 9 3 9 4 9 5

Practice writing numbers 91-100.

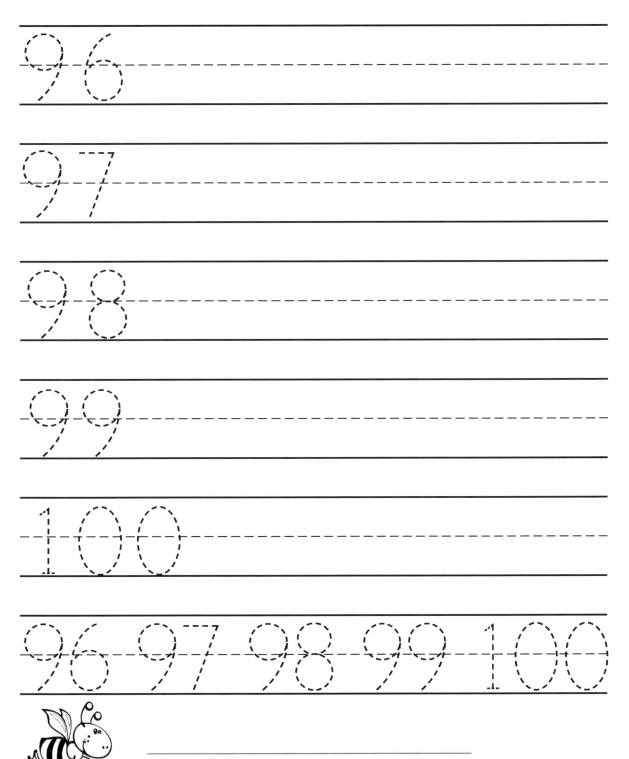

Trace and Write Numbers 1-100

Practice Review 51-100.

51 52 53 54

55 56 57 58

59 60 61 62

63 64 65 66

67 68 69 70

71 72 73 74 75

Practice Review 51-100.

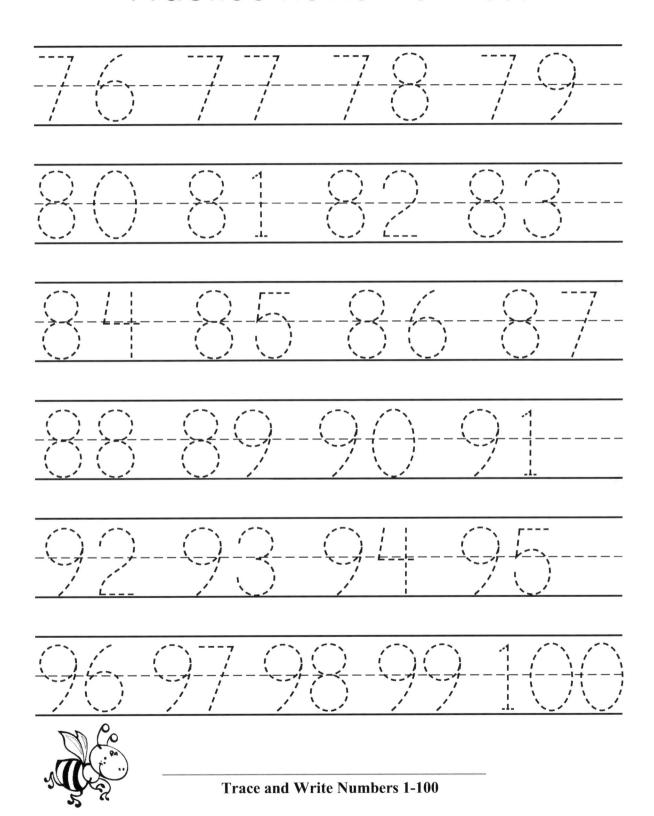

76 77 78 79

80 81 82 83

84 85 86 87

88 89 90 91

92 93 94 95

96 97 98 99 100

Trace and Write Numbers 1-100

PRACTICE REVIEW A
Numbers 1-100

Practice Review 1-100.

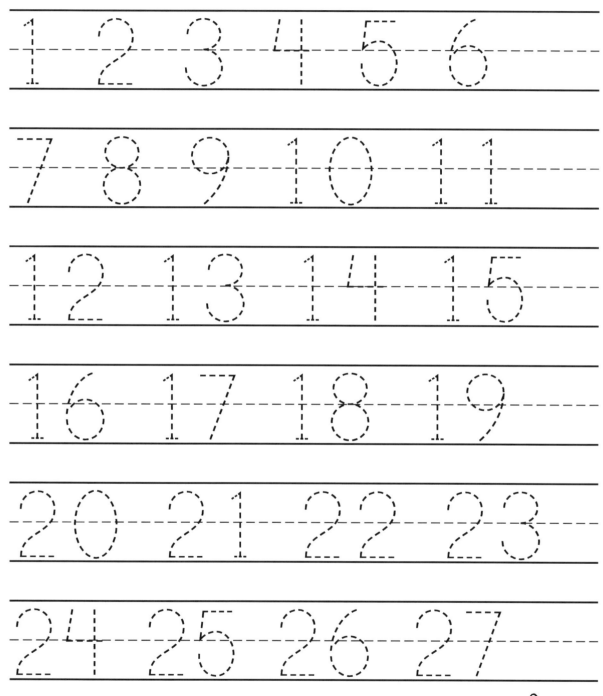

1 2 3 4 5 6

7 8 9 10 11

12 13 14 15

16 17 18 19

20 21 22 23

24 25 26 27

Trace and Write Numbers 1-100

Practice Review 1-100.

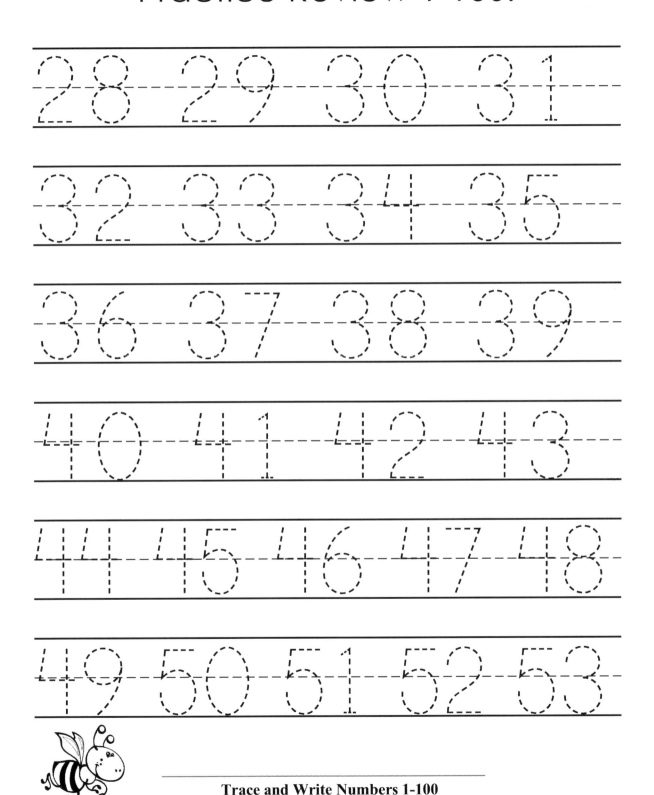

28 29 30 31

32 33 34 35

36 37 38 39

40 41 42 43

44 45 46 47 48

49 50 51 52 53

Trace and Write Numbers 1-100

Practice Review 1-100.

54 55 56 57

58 59 60 61

62 63 64 65

67 68 69 70

71 72 73 74

76 77 78 79

Practice Review 1-100.

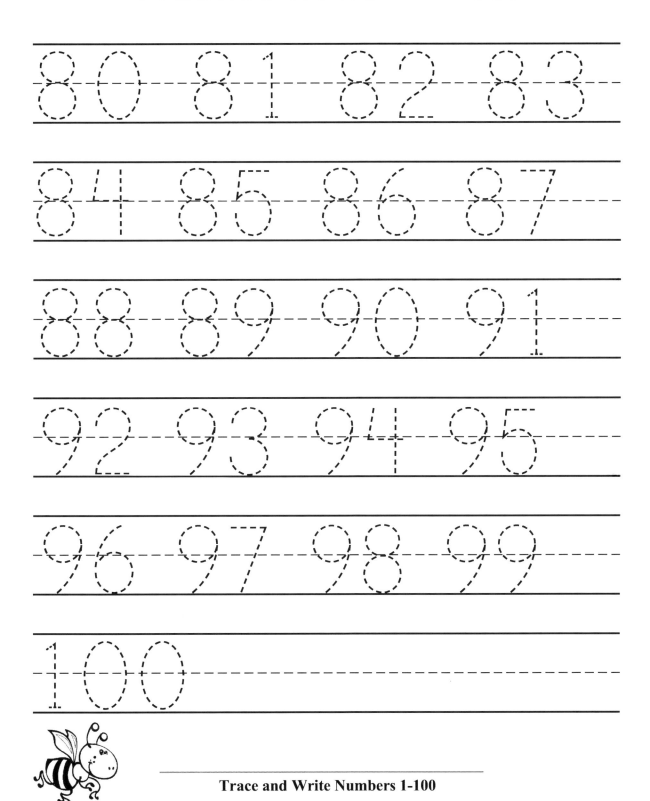

80 81 82 83
84 85 86 87
88 89 90 91
92 93 94 95
96 97 98 99
100

Trace and Write Numbers 1-100

Practice writing the numbers 1-100.

1

2

3

4

5

1 2 3 4 5

Practice writing numbers 1-100.

Trace and Write Numbers 1-100

Practice writing numbers 1-100.

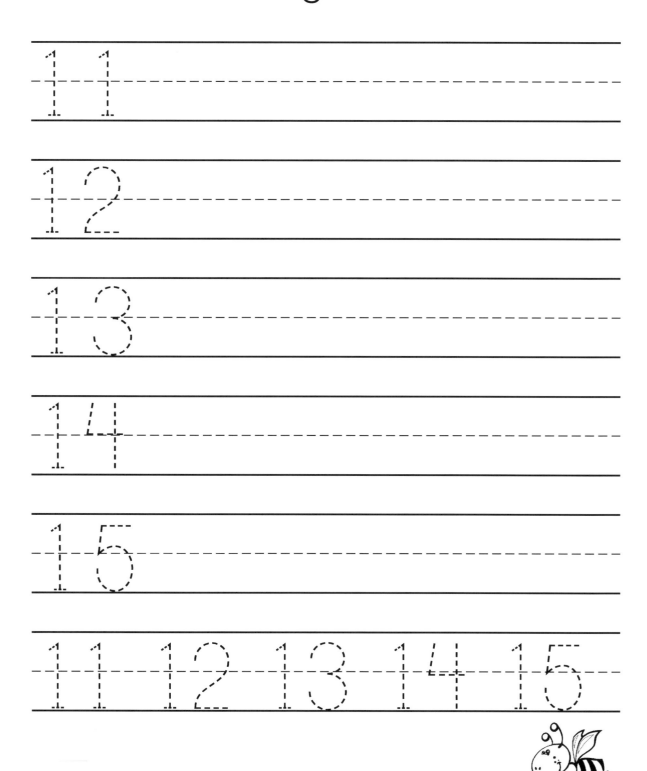

Practice writing numbers 1-100.

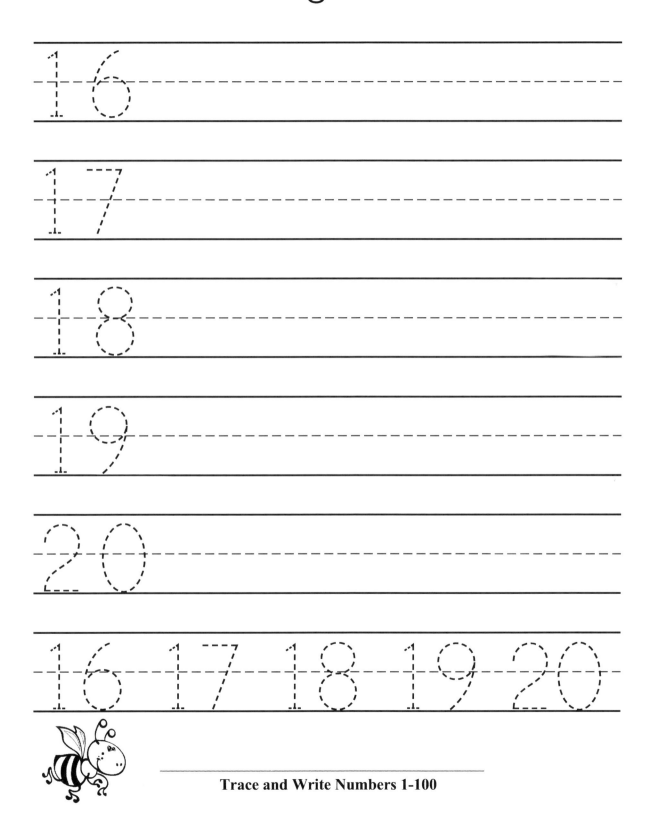

16

17

18

19

20

16 17 18 19 20

Trace and Write Numbers 1-100

Practice writing numbers 1-100.

21

22

23

24

25

21 22 23 24 25

Practice writing numbers 1-100.

Trace and Write Numbers 1-100

Practice writing numbers 1-100.

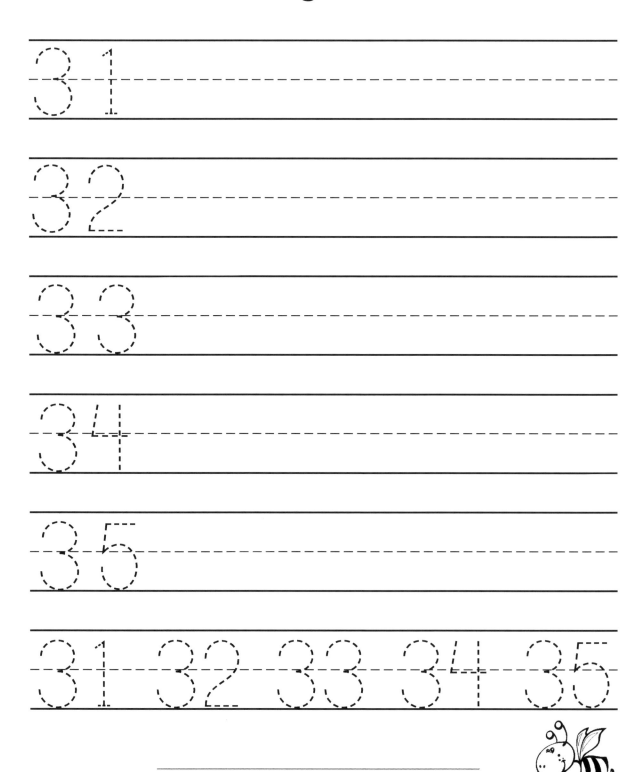

31

32

33

34

35

31 32 33 34 35

Trace and Write Numbers 1-100

Practice writing numbers 1-100.

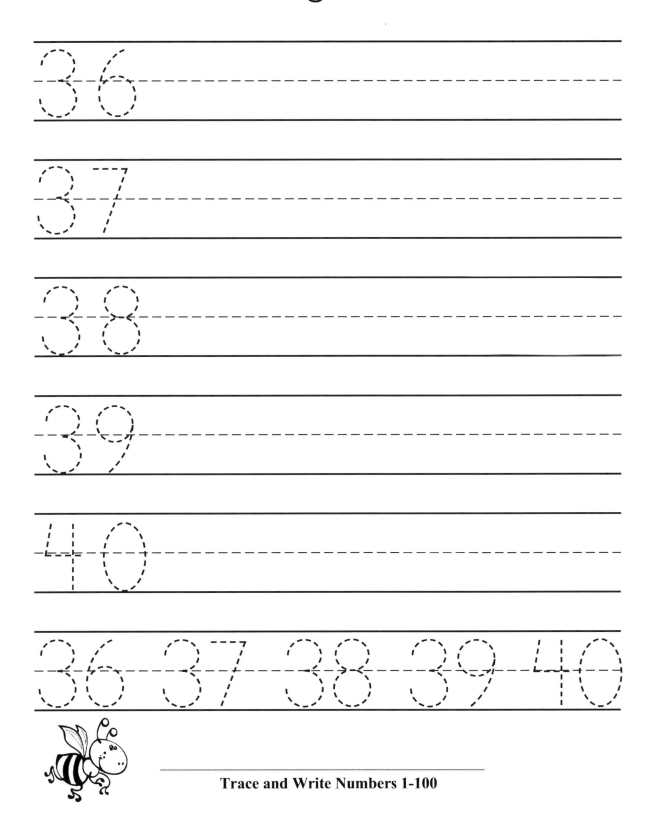

36

37

38

39

40

36 37 38 39 40

Trace and Write Numbers 1-100

Practice writing numbers 1-100.

4 1

4 2

4 3

4 4

4 5

4 1 4 2 4 3 4 4 4 5

Practice writing numbers 1-100.

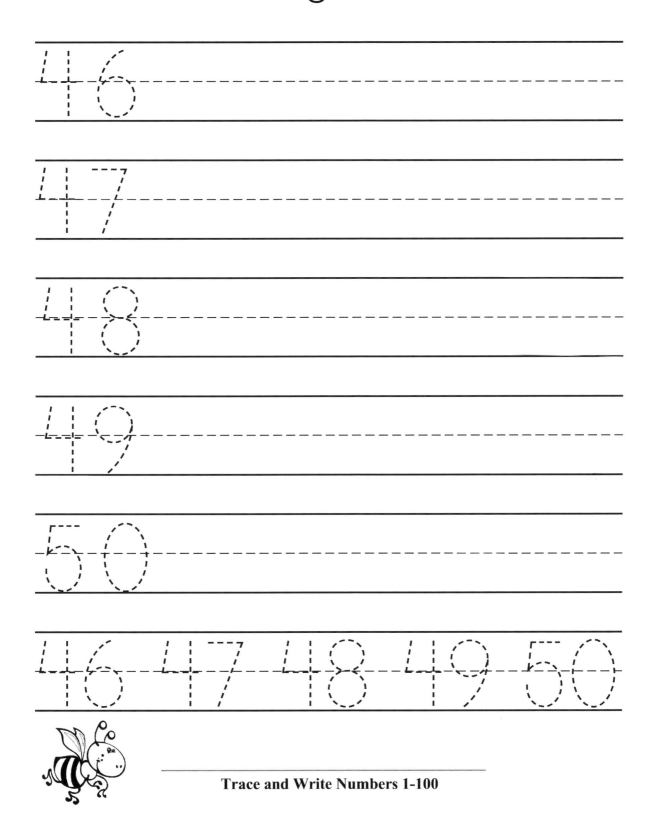

Trace and Write Numbers 1-100

Practice writing numbers 1-100.

51

52

53

54

55

51 52 53 54 55

Trace and Write Numbers 1-100

Practice writing numbers 1-100.

Practice writing numbers 1-100.

61 -

62 -

63 -

64 -

65 -

61 62 63 64 65

Practice writing numbers 1-100.

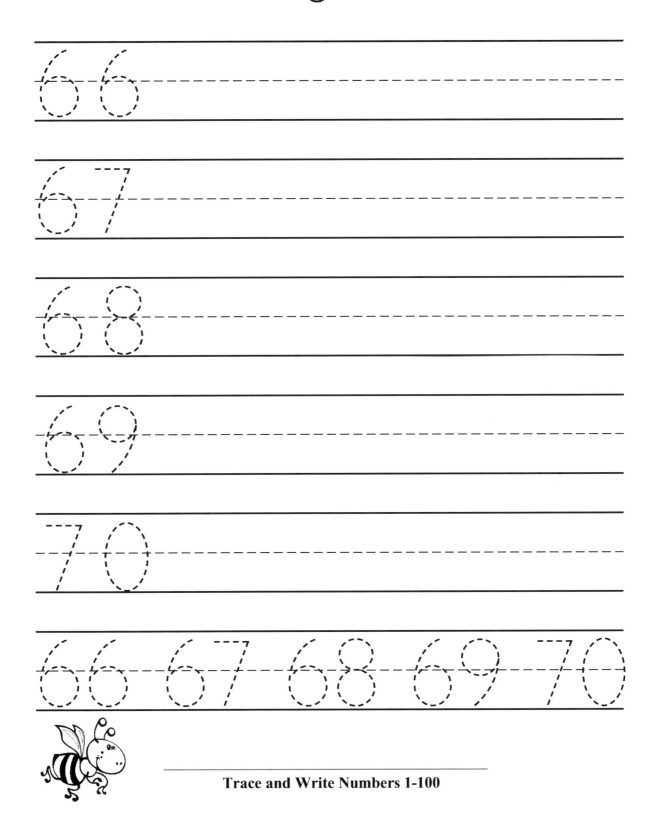

66

67

68

69

70

66 67 68 69 70

Trace and Write Numbers 1-100

Practice writing numbers 1-100.

7 1

7 2

7 3

7 4

7 5

71 72 73 74 75

Practice writing numbers 1-100.

76

77

78

79

80

76 77 78 79 80

Trace and Write Numbers 1-100

Practice writing numbers 1-100.

81

82

83

84

85

81 82 83 84 85

Practice writing numbers 1-100.

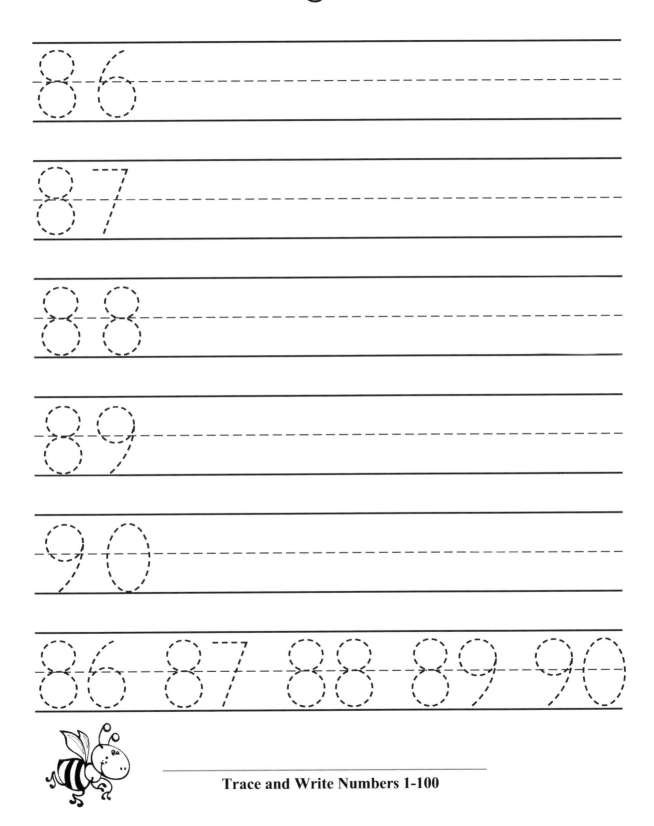

Trace and Write Numbers 1-100

Practice writing numbers 1-100.

9 1

9 2

9 3

9 4

9 5

9 1 9 2 9 3 9 4 9 5

Trace and Write Numbers 1-100

Practice writing numbers 1-100.

96

97

98

99

100

96 97 98 99 100

Trace and Write Numbers 1-100

Practice Review 1-100.

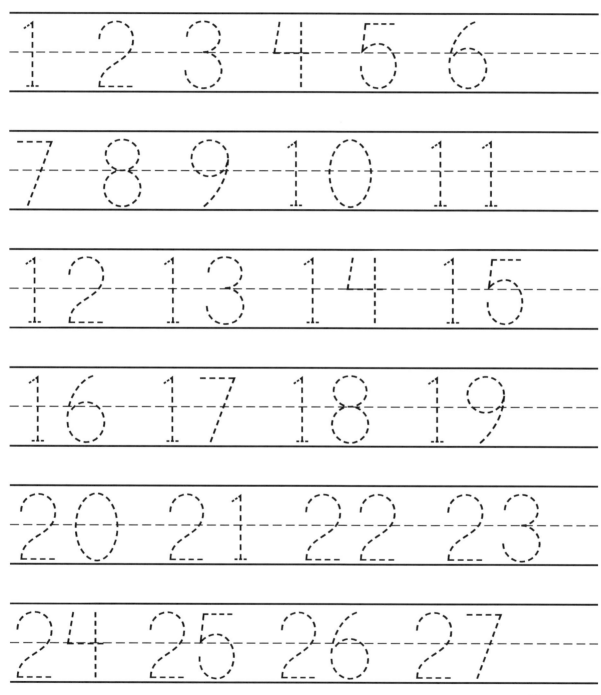

1 2 3 4 5 6

7 8 9 10 11

12 13 14 15

16 17 18 19

20 21 22 23

24 25 26 27

Trace and Write Numbers 1-100

Practice Review 1-100.

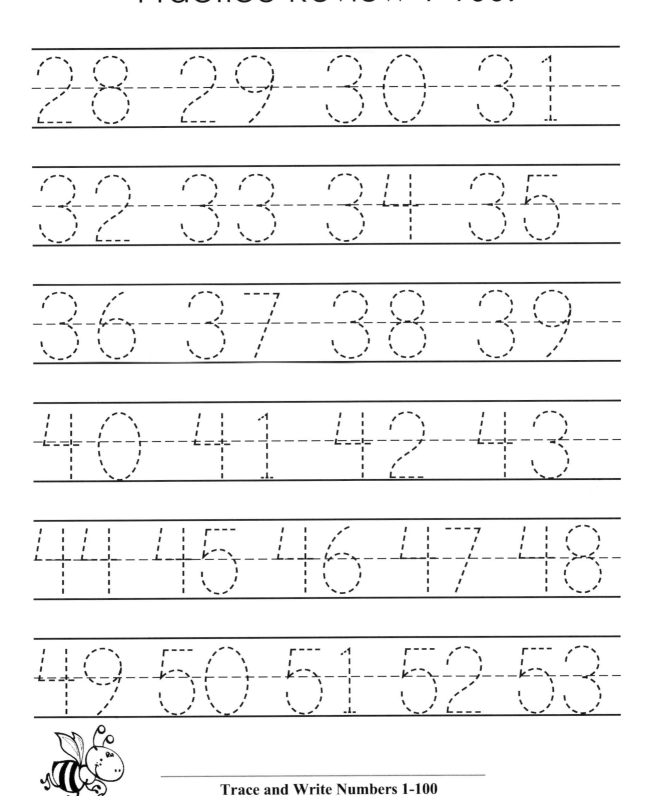

28 29 30 31

32 33 34 35

36 37 38 39

40 41 42 43

44 45 46 47 48

49 50 51 52 53

Trace and Write Numbers 1-100

Practice Review 1-100.

54 55 56 57

58 59 60 61

62 63 64 65

67 68 69 70

71 72 73 74

76 77 78 79

Practice Review 1-100.

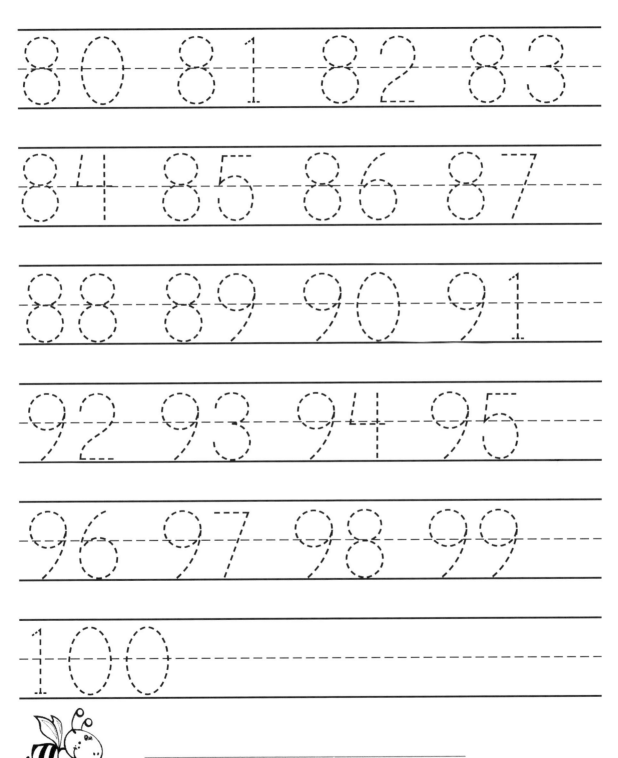

80 81 82 83

84 85 86 87

88 89 90 91

92 93 94 95

96 97 98 99

100

Trace and Write Numbers 1-100

Practice writing the numbers 1-100.

1

2

3

4

5

1 2 3 4 5

Trace and Write Numbers 1-100

Practice writing numbers 1-100.

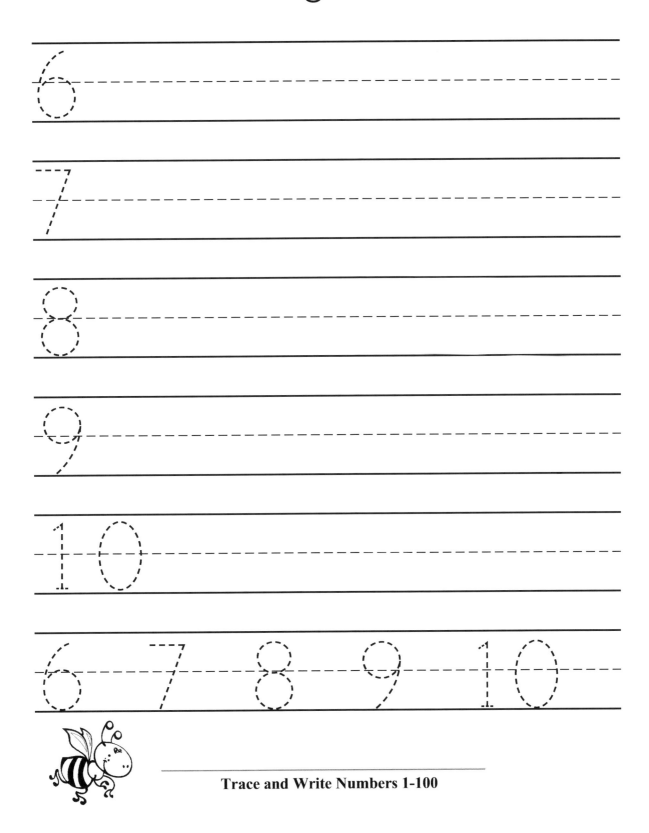

6

7

8

9

1 0

6 7 8 9 10

Trace and Write Numbers 1-100

Practice writing numbers 1-100.

11

12

13

14

15

11 12 13 14 15

Practice writing numbers 1-100.

16

17

18

19

20

16 17 18 19 20

Trace and Write Numbers 1-100

Practice writing numbers 1-100.

21

22

23

24

25

21 22 23 24 25

Trace and Write Numbers 1-100

Practice writing numbers 1-100.

26

27

28

29

30

26 27 28 29 30

Trace and Write Numbers 1-100

Practice writing numbers 1-100.

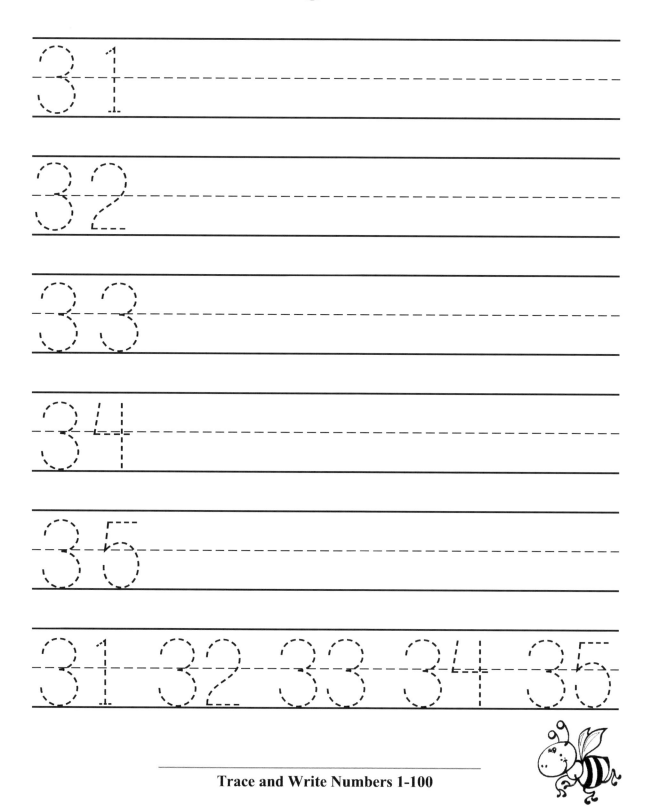

31

32

33

34

35

31 32 33 34 35

Practice writing numbers 1-100.

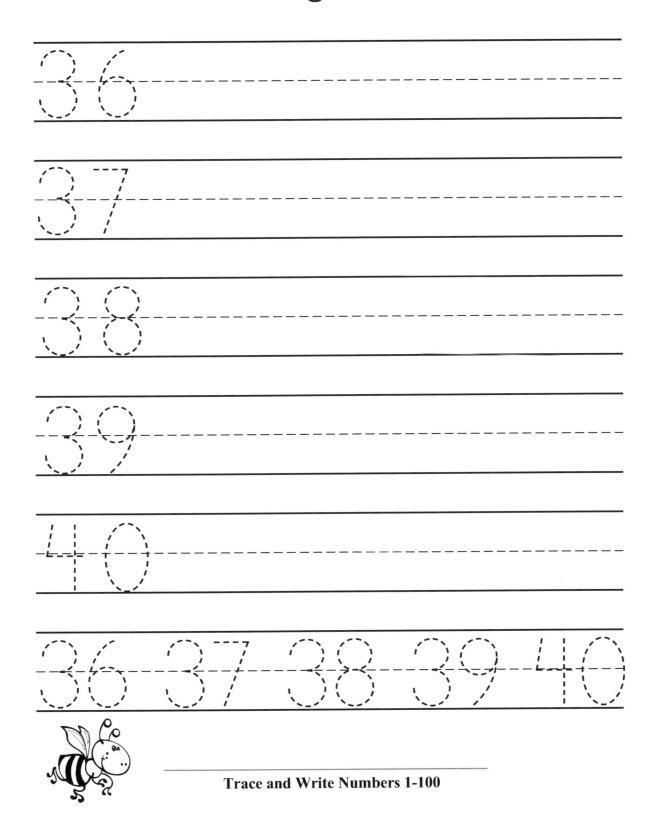

36

37

38

39

40

36 37 38 39 40

Trace and Write Numbers 1-100

Practice writing numbers 1-100.

41

42

43

44

45

41 42 43 44 45

Practice writing numbers 1-100.

Trace and Write Numbers 1-100

Practice writing numbers 1-100.

51

52

53

54

55

51 52 53 54 55

Trace and Write Numbers 1-100

Practice writing numbers 1-100.

5 6

5 7

5 8

5 9

6 0

5 6   5 7   5 8   5 9   6 0

Trace and Write Numbers 1-100

Practice writing numbers 1-100.

61

62

63

64

65

61 62 63 64 65

Practice writing numbers 1-100.

Trace and Write Numbers 1-100

Practice writing numbers 1-100.

71

72

73

74

75

71 72 73 74 75

Trace and Write Numbers 1-100

Practice writing numbers 1-100.

76

77

78

79

80

76 77 78 79 80

Practice writing numbers 1-100.

81

82

83

84

85

81 82 83 84 85

Practice writing numbers 1-100.

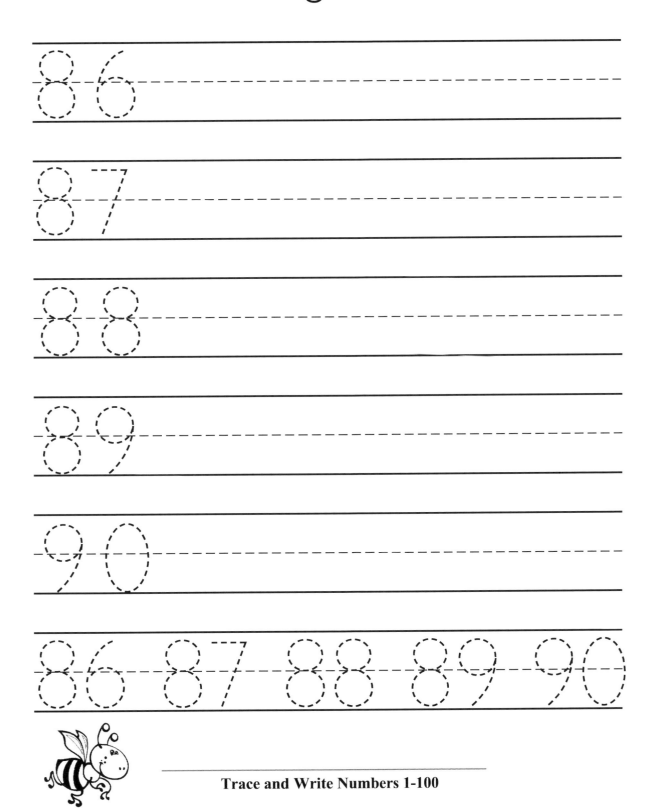

Trace and Write Numbers 1-100

Practice writing numbers 1-100.

91

92

93

94

95

91 92 93 94 95

Trace and Write Numbers 1-100

Practice writing numbers 1-100.

96

97

98

99

100

96 97 98 99 100

Trace and Write Numbers 1-100